Welcome
to the exciting world of
Perfect Paper Beads!

You don't need magical powers to transform sheets of colorful paper into fantastic beads—all you need are scissors and glue.

Making beads out of paper is a little-known technique, yet people have been creating beads this way for hundreds of years. Some Victorian jewelry was made with paper beads. Believe it or not, beads made from paper last a long time.

You can string paper beads to make necklaces, bracelets, earrings, ankle bracelets, and chokers. You can sew them to make a beaded purse or a vest fringed with beads. You can glue them to make greeting cards, pencil holders, and barrettes.

Use the beautiful paper included in this book–and other papers that you find or make–to create an amazing variety of perfect paper beads.

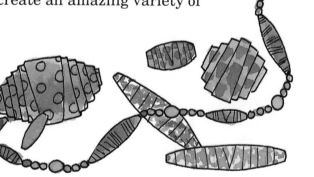

LET'S ROLL!

It's easy to get started rolling colorful beads out of paper. Here's what you'll need:

- Clean worktable—one you might get messy
- One sheet of beautiful paper (from the back of this book)
- Scissors
- Household glue
- Toothpicks
- Plate or tray to hold the beads
- Clear nail polish or acrylic varnish
- Lump of clay or Styrofoam cup

1. Cut along the dotted lines on your paper to get long triangles.
2. Place a toothpick on the bottom of a triangle. Pinch the end of the paper around the toothpick.

3. With your thumb and forefinger, roll the rest of the paper around the toothpick. Keep the paper centered and tight as you wind. But not too tight! You'll want to be able to slide the bead off the toothpick easily.
4. Put a dab of glue on the inside of the triangle's point. Press the bead between your thumb and forefinger. Use your other hand to turn the bead for about 30 seconds until it's secure.

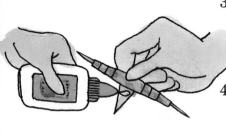

TIP Be sure not to get any glue on the wooden toothpick, or you won't be able to pull the bead off.

5. After the glue has dried (it takes about three minutes), to make beads durable coat them with clear nail polish or acrylic varnish. Hold the toothpick in one hand as you brush on clear nail polish or water-soluble acrylic varnish.

6. Stick the toothpick into a lump of clay or a Styrofoam cup to dry. Space out the toothpicks as you insert them. When the beads are dry to the touch (it takes about 1/2 hour), remove them from the toothpicks.

WARNING: WHEN USING NAIL POLISH OR VARNISH, ALWAYS WORK IN A WELL-VENTILATED AREA WITH AN ADULT CLOSE BY.

Secrets ... Write secret messages on the beads before you roll them up, and they'll become your own private time capsules. Write about your feelings, hopes, or goals–anything that will make you happy when you think of it inside your bead.

BEST FRIENDS

I love you

3

STRING THOSE BEADS!

You've rolled beads and you've coated them. Now it's time to string those beads into a fabulous necklace.

You'll need about 30 beads and a spool of nylon-coated wire. If you don't have wire, use a large, blunt needle and a spool of strong thread.

1. Push the wire or needle through the holes where the toothpicks were until you use up all the beads. Then measure the necklace around your neck to see if it is the length you want.

2. Unroll 4 more inches (10 cm) of wire or thread from the spool and cut. Tie the two ends together in a tight square knot. Now slip your necklace over your head. Doesn't it look terrific?

Snazzy paper makes snazzy beads. We've included several beautiful papers for you to use. But you can make paper beads out of any kind of paper—from paper bags and soup-can labels to beautiful wrapping papers and paper you paint yourself.

Colorful Paper from Magazines and Catalogs

Look through old magazines and catalogs for pictures with pretty colors. Ask permission, then carefully cut out the pages.

For truly colorful pages, eliminate printed words from magazine pages by swirling a permanent marker over the letters. Don't worry if the pages look messy. It won't be visible on the beads.

TIP An average-sized magazine page will make about 30 1-inch beads, 16 2-inch beads, or 6 3-inch beads.

Other Papers

Experiment with different kinds of paper to make beads.
- Wrapping paper—Festive beads
- Wallpaper—Designer beads
- Thick paper—Jumbo beads (See page 10.)
- Textured paper—Bumpy beads
- Newspaper—Black-and-white beads

PAINTED TO PERFECTION

Has Mom or Dad just dropped off all the magazines at the recycling center? Don't despair. You can still roll colorful beads by painting your own paper!

Marvelous Marbleizing

Paint paper to look like stone. Put a small amount of paint in a disposable container. Dip a sponge in the paint. Lightly pat the paper all over with the sponge. With a small paintbrush or cotton swab, swirl the paint around on the paper.

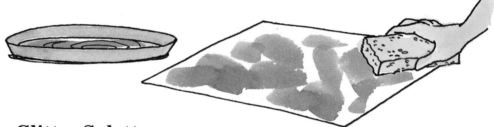

Glitter Splatter

Flick a paint-filled brush a few inches above paper. Let the paper dry. Splatter additional colors, letting each color dry between coats. Sprinkle on some glitter.

Perfect Patterns

Shapes: Draw or paint a design of colorful shapes.

Stripes: Horizontal and vertical stripes create different patterns on beads.

Dots: Make little dots with the point of your brush.

It's as easy as pie to cut your colorful paper into pie-shaped triangles. Here's how.

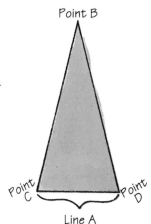

1. Decide how long you want your paper beads to be. Draw a line that length. For a 1-inch (2.5-cm) bead, lightly draw a line 1 inch (2.5-cm) long on your paper (line A).
2. Draw another line, twice as long, from the center of line A to point B. For a 1-inch (2.5-cm) bead, make this line 2 inches (5 cm) long.
3. Draw lines connecting point B to points C and D.
4. Cut out Triangle BCD. Measure and cut out other triangles from the paper the same way.

TIP Make various-sized triangles out of oaktag to use as patterns to trace on your paper.

Other Shapes

Changing the shape of the paper changes the shape of the bead.

- Straight rectangles make simple tube beads.
- Cutting paper with pinking shears adds a bumpy texture.
- To make a curved bead, string an uncoated bead on a piece of wire. Force the bead into a curve, brush it with acrylic, and allow it to dry overnight.

7

MIX AND MATCH

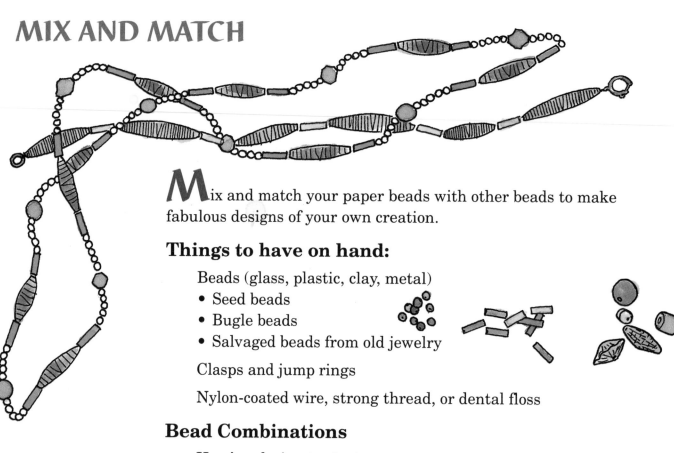

Mix and match your paper beads with other beads to make fabulous designs of your own creation.

Things to have on hand:

Beads (glass, plastic, clay, metal)
- Seed beads
- Bugle beads
- Salvaged beads from old jewelry

Clasps and jump rings

Nylon-coated wire, strong thread, or dental floss

Bead Combinations

Here's a design to start you on your way.

1. String a paper bead, then a bugle bead, then five seed beads.
2. Add a different bead (perhaps one you salvaged from an old necklace).
3. String five more seed beads, then another bugle bead.
4. Repeat steps 1-3 until you reach the desired length. Then tie off, depending on length, as explained on page 9.

How long should your necklace be? Loop some yarn or string around your neck to find the length you like best. A necklace that's too short to slip over your head will need a clasp.

Over-the-Head Necklaces

Use a combination of paper beads and other beads. Decide on your design before you start stringing. Then follow the basic directions on page 4.

TIP Tie the knot next to a paper bead, so you can slide the bead over the knot to conceal it.

Clasp Necklaces

If you're making a necklace that doesn't fit over your head, you'll need to tie a clasp to one end and a jump ring to the other end. Tie the clasp on before you begin. It will serve as a stopper while you're stringing.

1. Thread the small ring of the clasp, drawing all but 2 inches (5 cm) through. Tie with a double knot.
2. Dab clear nail polish onto the knot and trim the extra wire or string.
3. When you've strung on all the beads, double knot the jump ring to the other end. Dab clear nail polish onto the knot and trim the extra wire or string.

BIG BOLD BEADS!

Make some SUPER COLOSSAL JUMBO beads to wow your friends. To get the right look, you'll need heavier paper. The color doesn't matter because you'll color these beads *after* you make them. Use the same technique explained on pages 2-3, with these differences.

1. Use heavier, thicker paper. Try construction paper, drawing paper, oaktag, even thin cardboard.
2. Cut 2-1/2- (6-cm) by 5-inch (12.5-cm) triangles. Roll the triangles on a crochet needle or a similar long, rounded stick. If the triangles are too stiff to roll, dampen them first with a wet sponge. Allow beads to dry before continuing.
3. Draw designs on each bead with colorful markers or paints. Allow each color to dry before applying the next.
4. Hold each bead with the tip of a toothpick or pencil as you coat it with clear nail polish or varnish.

TIP Use regular-sized or jumbo beads to make the jewelry on the following pages. Or mix and match.

Chokers are short necklaces that hug your neck. Make several and give them as gifts. Your friends will hug you too!

Triple-strand Chokers

You'll need:
- Wire or thread
- 5 three-hole spacers of metal or wood (See illustration.)
- 18 1-inch (2.5-cm) paper beads
- 21 bugle beads
- Clasp and jump ring

1. Measure your neck with a piece of yarn. Then cut three pieces of wire or thread 3 inches (7.5 cm) bigger.
2. String wire through one bugle bead, one paper bead, and the top hole of a spacer. Repeat this pattern until you've used all the spacers, then add a bugle bead, a paper bead, and another bugle bead.

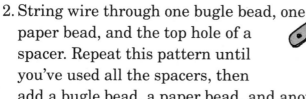
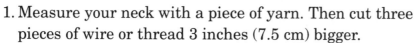

3. String the other pieces of wire the same way, threading them through the middle and bottom holes of the spacers.

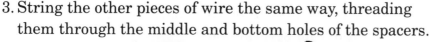

4. Knot the wires on both ends. Attach the clasp and jump ring.

13

BRILLIANT BARRETTES

Eyes will sparkle when you wear your brilliant barrette.

You'll need:
- Plain metal barrette
- About 8 to 16 1-inch (2.5-cm) paper beads, depending on the barrette's length
- Thin cardboard
- Paint and paintbrush
- All-purpose craft glue

1. Cut a strip of cardboard 1 inch (2.5 cm) wide and 1/4 inch (.6 cm) longer than the metal barrette.
2. Paint the cardboard to match the beads and let dry.
3. Glue a row of paper beads onto the painted side of the cardboard strip. Let dry.
4. Glue the bead-covered cardboard onto the metal barrette. Let it dry for several hours.

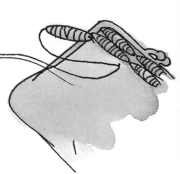

1 t's "sew" easy to make this terrific beaded purse.

You'll need:
- A plain cloth purse
- 1-1/2-inch (4-cm) paper beads—measure the purse to estimate the number of beads you'll need
- Threaded needle

1. Push the threaded needle from the inside of the material to the outside. Pull the thread all but 1 inch (2.5 cm) of the way through. Push the needle all the way back through the material at a point near the first hole. Tie the 1 inch (2.5 cm) of thread on the inside to the base of the thread on the needle. Double knot it.
2. Push the needle back to the outside of the material near the second hole. String a paper bead onto the needle, all the way to the base of the thread. Where the bead ends, push the needle back through the material to the inside.
3. Push the thread back through the material to the outside close to the last hole. Pull tight.
4. Repeat steps 2-3 until you've sewn on a complete row of beads. Begin a second row under the first. Continue until both sides of the bag are covered with beads. End with a double knot.

15

MORE GREAT IDEAS

Greeting Cards

Glue paper beads on homemade cards for a one-of-a-kind greeting. After the glue has dried, coat the beads with clear nail polish or varnish.

Pencil Holders

Glue paper beads onto clean empty cans to make pencil holders. Simply glue the beads down like mosaic tiles in any pattern that you wish. Let dry and coat with varnish.

Beaded Lampshades

Sew a fringe of paper and glass beads around the bottom of an old lampshade to brighten up a room.

Where to purchase supplies:

Many supplies needed for making jewelry can be mail-ordered. For a catalog, call or write:

Fire Mountain
28195 Redwood Hwy.
Cave Junction, OR 97523-9304
1 (800) 423-2319

Enterprise Art
P.O. Box 2918
Largo, FL 34649
1 (800) 366-2218